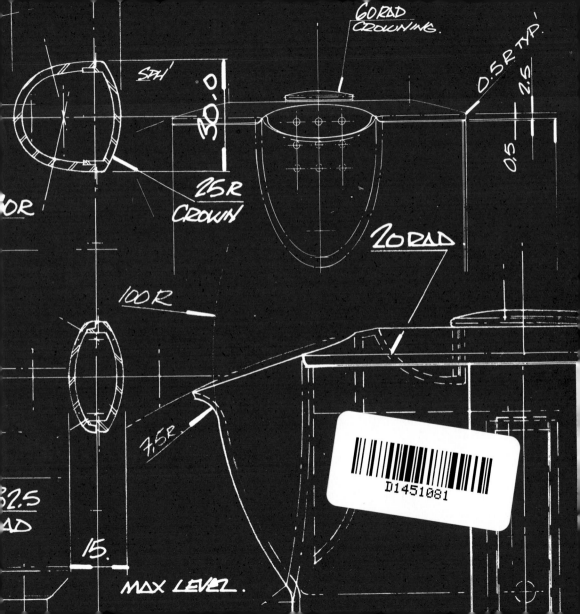

THE
KETTLE

THE

KETTLE

AN APPRECIATION

AURUM PRESS

JONATHAN M. WOODHAM ◉ PHOTOGRAPHS BY GUY RYECART

First published in Great Britain 1997 by
Aurum Press Limited, 25 Bedford Avenue,
London WC1B 2AT

A catalogue record for this book
is available from the British Library

ISBN 1 85410 527 2

This book was conceived,
designed and produced by
THE IVY PRESS LIMITED
2/3 St Andrews Place, Lewes,
East Sussex BN7 1UP

Art Director: Peter Bridgewater
Commissioning Editor: Viv Croot
Managing Editor: Anne Townley
Editors: Graham Smith, Julie Whitaker
Page layout: Ron Bryant-Funnell
Photography: Guy Ryecart

Printed and bound in China

Throughout this book the dimensions of
the objects are given in imperial and
metric measurements; height and width
are expressed by H and W.

22

15

12

23

29

16

25

20

11

24

27

19

11

31

26

22

17

14

19

30

12

16

31

29

23

13

10

18

21

26

15

14

25

21

28

Introduction

Cast-iron kettles were mass-produced in the 19th century and were generally sturdy, functional products, but by the turn of the century a number of designers were seeking to provide more refined solutions for water-heating. For example W.A.S. Benson, a late exponent of the Arts and Crafts movement, designed elegant kettles that were heated by a spirit burner underneath, and for safe and effortless pouring were fixed to

Hotpoint Premier
1925

stands by means of a pivot.

The introduction of electricity to the home made a significant impact on 20th-century design, although many pioneering kettles were simply recycled traditional designs with heating coils strapped to their undersides. These took about 12 minutes to boil one pint/600ml of water, and did little to encourage the widespread adoption of

Hotpoint
1925

AEG/Peter Behrens
1908-9

electric kettles, when gas rings could do the job more efficiently. The first attempt to produce a truly modern-looking product with consumer appeal was made by Peter Behrens, with his nickel-plated steel kettle designs for the progressive design-conscious German electricity company

Maddox
Late 1940s

of Allgemeine Electricitäts-Gesellschaft (AEG). However, it was the introduction of fully immersed heating elements that significantly speeded up the boiling of water, giving a considerable boost to the sales of electric models.

During the 1920s a number of avant-garde designers, particularly in Germany, began to explore the clean lines of the Modernist aesthetic in kettle designs, firmly imbuing them with a sense of *Zeitgeist* or 'spirit of the age'. Across the Atlantic, the USA saw a rapid expansion of the culture of domestic appliances, many of which took on the popular 'streamlined' styling features of the 1930s.

Bentink
Late 1930s

The postwar period brought many changes to people's lifestyles and aspirations. Automatic teamakers, such as the idiosyncratically designed Goblin Teasmade (first introduced in 1937), marked an increasing fascination with the idea of domestic automation. In the early 1950s, inbuilt automatic switches that cut out

at boiling point were increasingly introduced, replacing whistles, buzzers and other warning devices.

Other technological innovations changed the face of kettle design, including advances in pressed-steel fabrication and plastics technology. Polyacetal, a durable plastic that remained cool to the touch even when the water was boiling, was invented in the USA in 1958. It opened up radical new design possibilities in the form of the jug kettle, which, with its stylistic affinities with the coffee pot, began to develop fresh domestic markets.

Although there had been some design precedents, including ceramic jug kettles of the 1930s, the jug kettle did not take off significantly until the 1980s, when it was manufactured by a number of European and Japanese companies. Technological innovation was taken a step further in 1986 with the introduction of the first cordless kettle. By this time such models could boil two pints/1.2 litres of water in a little over three minutes.

Philips/Alessi
1995

In more affluent homes of the 1980s the kettle became the material embodiment of Post-Modernist aesthetics, a key element of the designer-influenced, equipment-conscious kitchen. A number of innovative companies, such as Alessi in Italy and Bodum in Switzerland, were prominent in this lucrative market niche. In such a context, the well-known adage 'a watched kettle never boils' became increasingly irrelevant, as status-conscious owners were ever-hopeful that their prized possession would simply be 'watched' or admired by visitors to their homes. The primary importance of kettles as objects of contemplation rather than function was borne out in a number of celebrated designs, most notably Starck's Hot Bertaa kettle, which carried a warning on its packaging: 'do not use when hot'!

Philippe Starck
1989

COPPER & BRASS, c.1900. H12 x W10.5IN / H30.5 x W26.5CM

W. A. S. BENSON

B ritish designer Benson was widely known for his stylish Arts and Crafts metalwork in copper and brass. This elegant, yet simple, design married practical needs to notions of refined living and afternoon tea in the drawing room. His work was much admired in France and Germany at the turn of the century. The slender, curvilinear handle and the form of the spout exhibit the organic feel of Art Nouveau.

BRASS, EARLY 1900S,
H13.75 X W13.24IN / H34.7 X W33.4CM

BRASS, 1908–9, H8.5 X W8IN / H21.5 X W20.5CM

JAN EISENLÖFFEL

First seen at the Turin Exhibition of 1902, variations of this Dutch kettle subsequently appeared in fashionable design shops, as well as decorative arts magazines and exhibitions in Germany and elsewhere. It has also been described as a chocolate kettle, catering for the making of a beverage popular in continental Europe. Whatever its use, it was not an object that could have been afforded by the everyday consumer gasping for a cup of tea.

AEG/PETER BEHRENS

A landmark in electrical product design, this was one of a range of mass-produced kettles in brass, nickel- and copper-plated brass designed by Behrens, who was brought into the AEG company in 1907 to modernize and coordinate its products, advertising and buildings. Such a clean-looking design solution reflected a genuine attempt to market a contemporary aesthetic in tune with the fresh production technologies offered by an innovative manufacturer.

MAGNET
GEC

Unlike the Behrens kettle, which sought to embrace the spirit of the 20th century, this rather staid, early electrical appliance relates far more closely to the traditional hob kettle. Very much embedded in the British way of life ('Don't worry, I'll just put the kettle on for a nice cup of tea'), this traditional shape has come to represent values of domesticity, cosiness and reassurance, particularly in times of crisis.

COPPER, C.1912, H8 X W7.5IN / H20.25 X W19CM

COPPER, C.1911,
H7.5 X W7IN / H19 X W17.75CM

PREMIER

A rather more elegant design solution than the almost contemporary GEC Magnet kettle, this largely unfussy British design was more in tune with the 'functional' aesthetic that was to become the hallmark of Modernist designers of the interwar years. Nonetheless, the traditional forms of the handle of both kettle and lid tied it as much to the past as to its present or future.

COPPER, C. 1620, H8 X W12IN / H20.25 X W30.5CM

SPECIAL KETTLE
BELLING

This rather eccentric-looking British kettle had a flat, square base designed to make maximum contact with the hot plate of the electric cookers on which it was intended to sit. The very fact that its design was closely tied to the kitchen may account for its somewhat basic general appearance. The rather odd, downward-pointing spout must have made it extremely difficult to pour, particularly if the kettle was full.

NICKEL-PLATED STEEL, C.1920'
H9 X W8IN / H22.75 X W20.25CM

HOTPOINT
EDISON ELECTRIC APPLIANCE CO.

This rather fanciful 'Aladdin's lamp' shape assumed the voguish vocabulary of Art Deco that became popular in both Europe and the United States in the 1920s. Although the forms of the handle and body were in tune with the exotic sources upon which many contemporary Art Deco designers drew, the prosaic spout remained an indelicate reminder of the product's straightforward functional role.

NICKEL-PLATED COPPER, C.1925,
H8 X W8.5IN / H20.25 X W21.5CM

ABC

The angular twelve-sided design of this German kettle, together with the rather chunky knob of the lid and twin decorative bands encircling the body, reflected the fashionable geometric forms of Art Deco. Nonetheless, in many other respects – such as the spout and handle – it remains more closely tied to tradition than the earlier Behrens kettle for AEG.

PREMIER ACCIDENT PROOF

Building on the company's pre-First World War models, this design shows that, for many consumers, technological improvements were as important as ephemeral styling. Its basic safety cut-out mechanism anticipated the widespread incorporation of similar, but more sophisticated mechanisms that allowed users to finish reading the paper, answer the telephone or hang out the washing without worring about the kettle boiling dry.

COPPER, C.1925,
H10 X W9.75IN / H25.5 X W24.75CM

UNIVERSAL TEA BALL TEAPOT
LANDERS, FRARY & CLARK

The American-made Universal clearly borrowed the form of a pot designed for coffee, a widely consumed beverage in the USA. Although largely undecorated, the geometric forms of the lid and handle have an Art Deco flavour. Like the Hotpoint kettle, this tea-kettle would have sat more easily on the fashionable breakfast table than out of sight in the kitchen.

CHROMIUM-PLATED BRASS, C.1926,
H9.5 X W9IN / H24 X W22.75CM

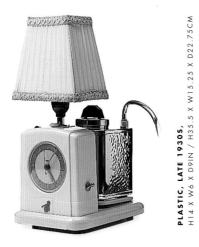

PLASTIC, LATE 1930S,
H14 X W6 X D9IN / H35.5 X W15.25 X D22.75CM

TEASMADE

GOBLIN

In 1937 the Goblin company began manufacturing automatic teamakers, extraordinary bedside devices that were meant to awaken their owners with an alarm call and a fresh cup of tea – assuming, of course, that they could actually have slept through the gurgling and spluttering noises that the machines made when in operation. This popular wedding present was a gadget of which Heath Robinson would have been proud.

CHROME-STEEL &
BAKELITE, LATE 1930S'
H8.5 X W12IN
H21.5 X W30.5CM

BENTINK

HMV/CHRISTIAN BARMAN

Barman, a leading design journalist as well as a designer, was well known for his work for HMV. This striking design has a somewhat aerodynamic feel in the subtly rounded form of the body and flowing lines of the handle, and is a rather restrained – and very British – acknowledgement of the streamlined forms that dominated the US appliance market of the time.

SPEEDIE KETTLEJUG

The flowing lines of this rather elegant design anticipated the interest in organic form that excited many designers in Italy and the USA in the postwar years. It also anticipated the popularity of kettle jugs in the 1980s, when these were rendered very much more practical by the invention of new plastics. However, the safety aspects of this particular model left something to be desired, as it had a bare-wired immersed heating element!

TECAL
HAWKINS

Like the rival Teasmade, this rather austere design boiled water in a chrome kettle. The hot water dripped out of the tube-like spout straight onto tea leaves in a pot, which, together with cups and a jug of milk, had been prepared the night before, realizing the proud owner's dream of automated living. The traditional tasselled lampshade is an attempt to harmonize the teamaker with its bedroom surroundings.

MADDOX

HMV

CHROMIUM-PLATED STEEL &
BAKELITE, LATE 1940S,
H8 X W9.5IN
H20.25 X W24.25CM

This kettle was typical of British design in the immediate postwar years – practical-looking with an aura of neatness and efficiency. Something of a compromise shape between a coffee percolator and a teapot, its functional aesthetic anticipated the design restraint of many later plastic jug kettles. Its look was maybe too 'different' to catch on at the time.

SWAN BRAND

BULPITT & SONS

This highly functional electric kettle made few concessions to styling, combining a very traditional kettle form with an immersion element. The simplicity of the design reflected the 1940s' Utility programme, a state-imposed scheme for consumer goods that favoured simple, soundly constructed and durable products. A typically 'no-nonsense' and quintessentially British kettle, it was coated in brown 'Wartime Finish'.

LATE 1950S, H7.5 X W8.5IN, STEEL & BAKELITE, H19 X W21.5CM

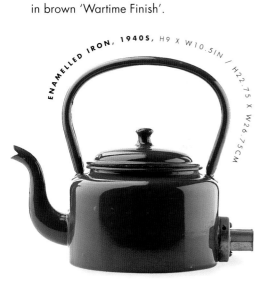

ENAMELLED IRON, 1940S, H9 X W10.5IN / H22.75 X W26.75CM

NEW MAID

Finished in a variety of coloured metallized finishes, this classic British design anticipated a number of 1980s' Post-Modern products such as the Japanese K600 Horn kettle by Yoshira Fuwa. As with many British designs, the New Maid was firmly anchored in practicalities: the heavy base ensured stability, while the handle was kept well clear of the hot steam from the spout. Its shrill and piercing two-tone whistle contrasts with the deeper, more sophisticated tones of Sapper's 1983 Alessi kettle.

STEEL, LATE 1950S.
H9 X W10.5IN
H22.75 X W26.75CM

MONOGRAM SIMMERMATIC

GK10

A very much more self-consciously styled product than the New Maid, the Simmermatic also exhibited a more technologically sophisticated aesthetic. Its solid, yet unfussy, appearance and clean profile were less subject to the vagaries of ephemeral styling than many of its competitors, perhaps suggesting to would-be purchasers that it was both a more durable and more functionally efficient product, representing good value for money.

KRUPS

This highly stylized model looks, in profile, much like a helmet from a Buck Rogers' movie. Its design reflected the general public's desire to own domestic appliances that looked as if they embodied 'state-of-the-art' technology, even if, in reality, their performance had little to distinguish them from their competitors.

SIREN
SWAN

The Siren could only be filled (or poured) by means of a trigger mechanism that raised the whistle, thus anticipating Sapper's later, but equally uncomfortable, finger-scalding design for Alessi. With its US-style streamlined body, handle and spout, the Siren represented, to prospective British purchasers, the consumer paradise glimpsed in US films, television programmes and magazines.

ACETAL & STAINLESS STEEL, 1973,
H8.25 X W11IN / H21 X W28CM

FUTURA

RUSSELL HOBBS/JULIUS THALMANN

This kettle, with its smoothly contoured profile, was developed from an awareness of the moulding possibilities of thermoplastics. Although stylistically something of a hybrid between an avant-garde curling-stone and a science-fiction image from the period, the Futura offered a number of practical advantages – it was lightweight and boasted a water-level indicator.

POLYTHENE, 1976,
H9.25 X W11.5IN / H23.5 X W29.25CM

POWERSPEED

This rather aerodynamic-looking design was contemporary with popular science-fiction visions of the future, such as *Star Trek, 2001: A Space Odyssey,* and *The Star Wars* trilogy. Unfortunately, despite its futuristic styling and cool colouring, it has proved rather less enduring than its cinematic counterparts.

AGALUXE

This highly traditional design shows the enduring fascination for nostalgia in the home. Designed at a time when interest in heritage was growing, the Aga kettle embraced the highly fashionable values that were compatible with the increasingly popular 'farmhouse kitchen' image. Though primarily made for owners of Aga cookers, its appeal was far more widespread.

ALESSI/RICHARD SAPPER

Designed to be seen and heard (the bronze whistle emits two deep notes that have been likened to those on Amtrak locomotives), this kettle became a fashionable cult icon in the 1980s, when a conspicuous display of stylish domestic appliances and cookware was a key element in 'designer lifestyling'. However, the rather uncomfortable polyamide-coated handle, and the often painfully hot lever for raising the spout-lid, necessitated physical concessions in the cause of fashionable living.

ALUMINIUM, 1978,
H10.5 X W10.5IN
H26.75 X W26.75CM

BIRD KETTLE

ALESSI/MICHAEL GRAVES

American Michael Craves is a leading Post-Modernist architect who worked for design companies widely celebrated for the creation of aesthetically charged, expensive tableware, furniture, interiors and kitchenware. His kettle caught the imagination of many fasion-conscious consumers of the 1980s. The bird-sharped whistle, complete with shrill 'song' when boiling, both lent the kettle its name and typified the so-called 'wit' of much Post-Modernist design.

STAINLESS STEEL, 1985,
H8.75 X W10.25IN / H22 X W26CM

POLYPROPYLENE, 1986,
H10.25 X W4.75IN / H26 X W12CM

GEOFF HOLLINGTON
HOLLINGTON ASSOCIATES

Jug kettles captured an increasingly significant sector of the kettle market during the 1980s. This example is typical of the new breed, exploring the formal possibilities afforded by innovations in plastics technology. The move towards the coffee-pot aesthetic also helped manufacturers to penetrate fresh markets in non-tea-drinking European countries.

OTTONI MODEL 5020
BODUM/CARSTEN JORGENSEN

This was the first kettle designed for Bodum, combining practicality (as exemplified by the non-heat-conducting wooden handle) with elegance and high-quality manufacture. The gold-plated hinges and top contrast with the highly polished stainless-steel body and Pacific-blue knob, while the studs subtly enrich the surface, rather in the manner of those on Graves' Bird kettle.

STAINLESS STEEL, 1986,
H8 X W7.75IN / H20.25 X W19.75CM

IL CONICO
ALDO ROSSI

This elegant and minimalist statement is in keeping with the fashionable interest in the concept of Micro-Architecture, whereby many small-scale table-top products were designed with architectonic principles in mind. Nonetheless, Il Conico's significance is greater as a cultural icon than a really practical everyday solution to the boiling of water.

HOT BERTAA
ALESSI/PHILIPPE STARCK

Highly sculptural, this kettle has been widely criticized for its emphasis on styling at the expense of function. It is heavy and awkward to fill, seen to be full only when water overflows from the spout, known to be boiling only when billowing steam, unsafe to pick up when hot without a protective cloth and difficult to pour. Nonetheless, it marks the compelling metamorphosis of a humdrum object into an aesthetically resonant fashion statement by France's most celebrated designer of the 1980s.

POLYPROPYLENE, C. 1990, H10 X W9.25IN / H25.25 X W23.5CM

SEASONS K4

RUSSELL HOBBS

Able to be filled without unplugging the electrical connection, this unfussy design was typical of many cordless models that captured an increasingly large share of the domestic market. Its somewhat rugged aesthetic is ideal for everyday use and easily distinguished from the more obviously stylish jug kettles designed for Philips, Alessi and Bodum.

STAINLESS STEEL, 1992, H7 X W9.75IN / H18 X W25CM

PITO
ALESSI/FRANK GEHRY

A playful visual pun on the term 'fish kettle', this is another of the Italian Alessi company's 'designer' kettles that owes more to artistic licence than to practicality. The flying-fish motif for the whistle, the organic handle and the lop-sided conical form are sculptural elements of an object that is surely designed to be talked about as much as used.

STAINLESS STEEL, 1992, H8.5 X W8.25IN / H21.5 X W21CM

OSIRIS
BODUM/CARSTEN JÖRGENSEN

This is a rather eloquent example of Late Modernism but for the rather whimsical brackets supporting the handle. The Osiris is very much part of the 'designer lifestyling' of the period, equally at home in design museums, expensive kitchenware stores and the pages of glossy magazines. It also boils water!

IBIS
BODUM/CARSTEN JÖRGENSEN

Made in polypropylene with a stainless-steel heating element, the Ibis range came in a variety of colours. This translucent model epitomizes the understated elegance of much Danish design, coordinating neatly with other Bodum domestic products, such as the ubiquitous French-style cafetières. It is also efficient, boiling 12 cupfuls of water in in a matter of 4.5 minutes.

POLYPROPYLENE, 1992,
H10.5 X W8.75IN / H26.5 X W22.25CM

POLYPROPYLENE, C.1994,

H9 X W8.5IN / H22.75 X W21.5CM

KENWOOD /KENNETH GRANGE

The curvilinear profile of the handle, lid and underside of the spout are an attempt to breathe life into the generally prosaic form of the jug kettle, without compromising its aura of straightforward, functional efficiency. Grange's kettle exhibits the economy of form and detailing that have characterized his designs for several decades.

PHILIPS/ALESSI

The complex textured surfaces of this design-conscious kettle were modelled by computer at the English plant at Hastings. Using such sophisticated tools, designers have considerable expressive, yet practical, possibilities at their disposal. Almost cockatoo-like in profile, this stylish kettle can boil 1 3/4 pints/one litre of water in 3.5 minutes.

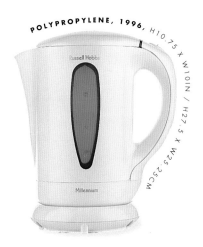

POLYPROPYLENE, 1996, H10.75 X W10IN / H27.5 X W25.25CM

POLYPROPYLENE, 1995,
H10.5 X W10IN / H26.5 X W25.25CM

MILLENNIUM
RUSSELL HOBBS

This product was advertised as 'the most advanced kettle in the world', bringing the consumer 'tomorrow's technology today'. One of the fastest-boiling kettles available, it is heated by a flat disc-shaped element, an innovation also designed to cut down on limescale deposits. The cordless version can be plugged in at any angle on the base, thus also making it suitable for left- or right-handed use. As with many products geared to global markets, technological innovation is as important as appearance.

ACKNOWLEDGEMENTS

The publishers would like to thank the following for the loan of kettles for photography:

Amberley Museum, Arundel, West Sussex: page 11 right; 12 left and right; 13; 14 left and right; 15 left and right; 17 left; 19 left; 21 right

Bodum, Covent Garden: page 25 right; 29 left

Paul Clark: page 29 right

Design Goes Pop, Manchester: page 16 right; 18; 19 right; 20; 21 left; 22 left and right; 31 left and right

Kenneth Grange at Pentagram: page 30, endpapers

Hoad and Taylor, Haywards Heath: page 23 left

Russell Hobbs: page 27

Hollington Associates: page 25 left

The Royal Pavilion Art Gallery and Museum, Brighton: page 10; 23 right; 24

Enrico Tedeschi: page 16 left; 17 right

The publishers would like to thank the following for the use of pictures:

Alessi: page 26 left and right

Norman Black: page 28

The British Museum: page 11 left. Copyright © British Museum

Endpapers: working drawing for Kenwood kettle courtesy of Pentagram Design Limited

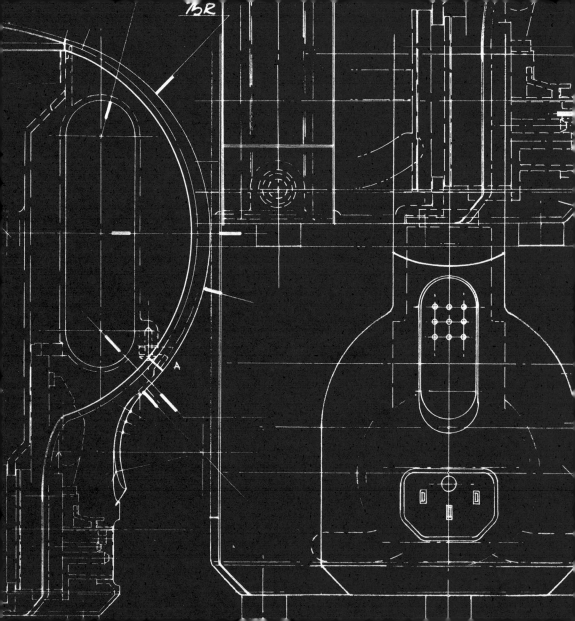